Thank you for bringing our coloring books to life with your creativity and enthusiasm. Please share your feedback and ideas for new content, as your insights are invaluable in shaping our future creations.

Happy Coloring!

Made in the USA
Las Vegas, NV
07 February 2024

85465380R00085